MW00563697

Detail of arch design, Gallery of Apollo, Louvre

FRENCH ARCHITECTURAL ORNAMENT

From Versailles, Fontainebleau and Other Palaces

Edited by
EUGÈNE ROUYER

DOVER PUBLICATIONS, INC.
Mineola, New York

Copyright

Bibliographical Note

This Dover edition, first published in 2007, is a new selection of 91 plates containing 161 designs in both color and black and white. The black-and-white plates have been selected from *L'art architectural en France depuis François Ier jusqu'à Louis XIV.* (2 vols.) by Eugène Rouyer, originally published by Noblet et Baudry, Paris, in 1863–66. The sixteen color plates are from *La peinture décorative en France du XVIe au XVIIIe siècle* by P. Gélis-Didot, originally published by C. Schmid, Paris, in 1897–99; and unidentified sources.

Library of Congress Cataloging-in-Publication Data

French architectural ornament from Versailles, Fontainebleau and other palaces / edited by Eugène Rouyer.
p. cm.
"A . . . selection of 92 plates containing 161 designs in both color and black and white. The black-and-white plates have been selected from L'art architectural en France depuis François Ier jusqu'à Louis XIV. (2 vols.) by Eugène Rouyer, originally published by Noblet et Baudry, Paris, in 1863–66. The sixteen color plates are from La peinture décorative en France du XVIe au XVIIIe siècle by P. Gélis-Didot, originally published by C. Schmid, Paris, in 1897–99; and unidentified sources."
ISBN-13: 978-0-486-46140-3
ISBN-10: 0-486-46140-8
1. Decoration and ornament, Architectural—France. 2. Mural painting and decoration, French. I. Rouyer, Eugène, 1827–1891. II. Rouyer, Eugène, 1827–1891. Art architectural en France depuis François Ier jusqu'à Louis XVI. Selections. III. Gélis-Didot, Pierre, 1853– Peinture décorative en France du XVIe au XVIIIe siècle. Selections.

NA3549.A1F73 2007
729.0944—dc22

2007023382

Manufactured in the United States of America
Dover Publications, Inc., 31 East 2nd Street, Mineola, N.Y. 11501

PLATE 1. Fireplace wall, salon of Diane, Versailles

PLATE 2. Salon of Diane, Versailles

Plate 3. War room, Versailles

PLATE 4. Details from war room, Versailles

PLATE 5. Carved wooden door, Versailles

Plate 6. Lead fountain, Versailles

PLATE 7. Lead vases in Neptune fountain, Versailles

Plate 8. Ceiling of the queen's bedroom, Versailles

PLATE 9. Detail of ceiling in queen's bedroom, Versailles

PLATE 10. Door to queen's bedroom, Versailles

PLATE 11. Queen's bedroom (details), Versailles

PLATE 12. Fireplace wall, Versailles

PLATE 13. Decorative mirror on wall, Versailles

PLATE 14. Window wall, Versailles

PLATE 15. Ceiling plan, Versailles

PLATE 16. Various details, Versailles

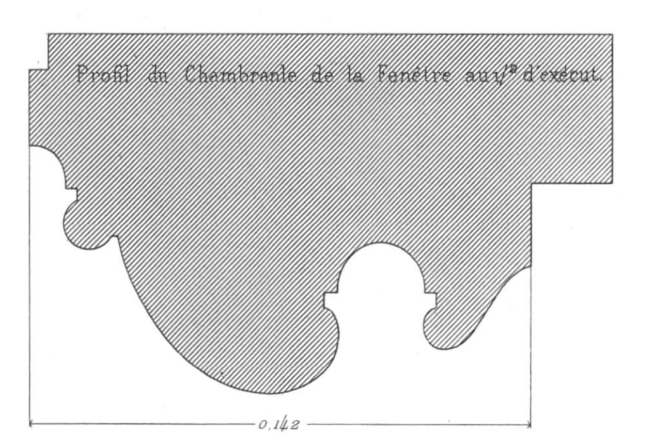

Plate 17. Various details, Versailles

PLATE 18. Detail of arch, Gallery of Apollo, Louvre

Plate 19. Detail of arch, Gallery of Apollo, Louvre

PLATE 20. Door, Gallery of Apollo, Louvre

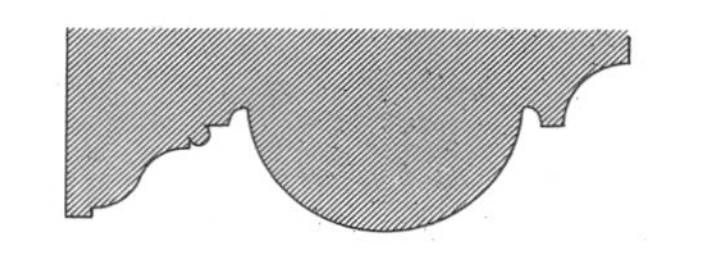

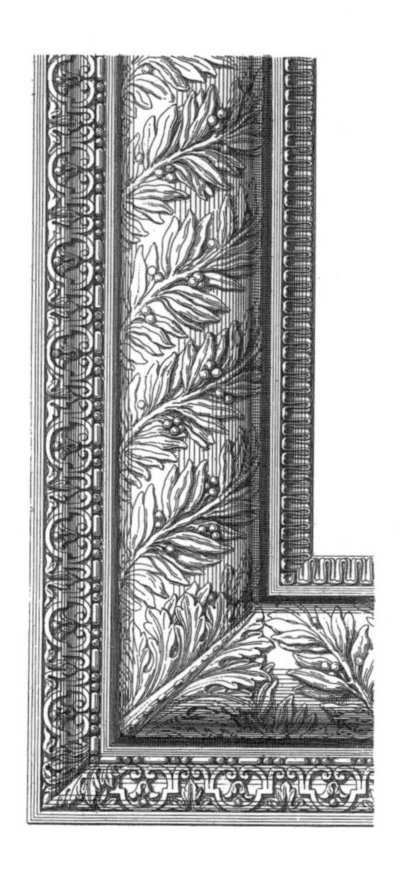

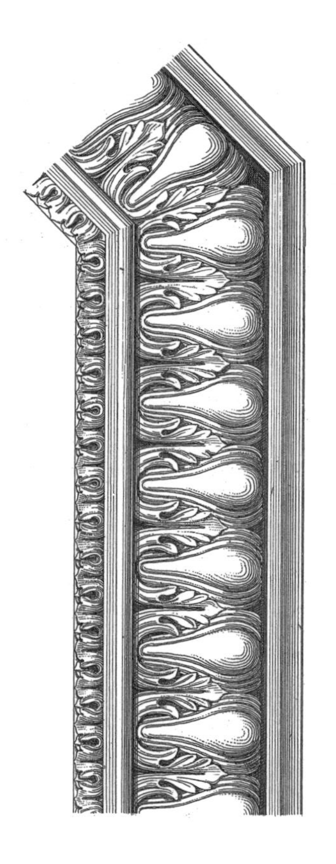

Plate 21. Details, Gallery of Apollo, Louvre

PLATE 22. Ceiling of an alcove in Henri IV's bedroom, Louvre

Plate 23. Bedroom of the Duchesse d'Etampes, Fontainebleau

Plate 24. Doorway of Anne of Austria's Salon, Fontainebleau

PLATE 25. Details of Anne of Austria's Salon, Fontainebleau

PLATE 26. Portion of ceiling, Anne of Austria's Salon, Fontainebleau

Plate 27. Ceiling details, Anne of Austria's Salon, Fontainebleau

Plate 28. Ceiling of the queen's library, Chateau de Chenonceaux

Plate 29. Decorative ornaments, Fontainebleau

PLATE 30. Fontainebleau

PLATE 31. Fontainebleau

PLATE 32. Doorway, Fontainebleau

PLATE 33. Stairway decoration, Fontainebleau

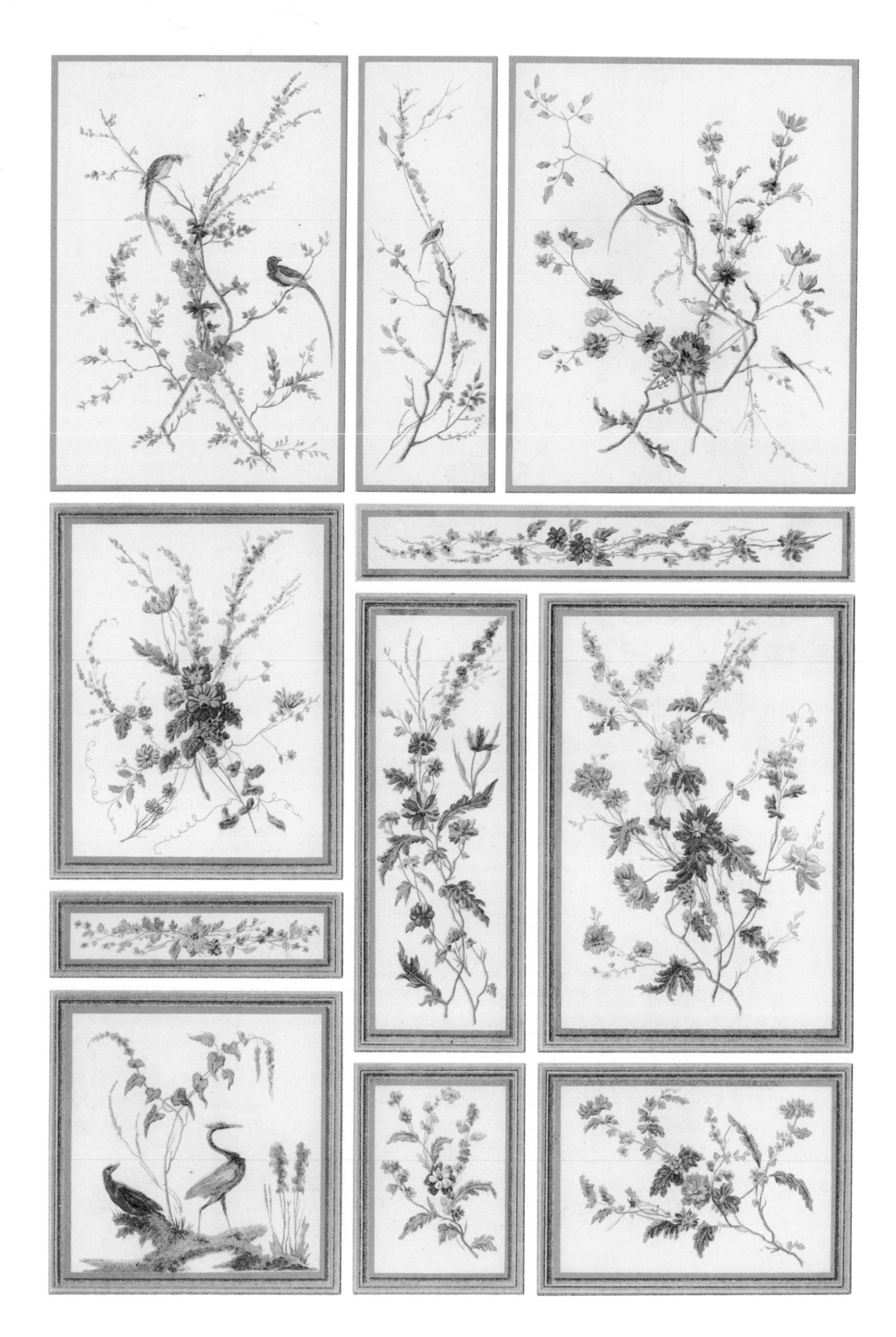

PLATE 34. Fontainebleau

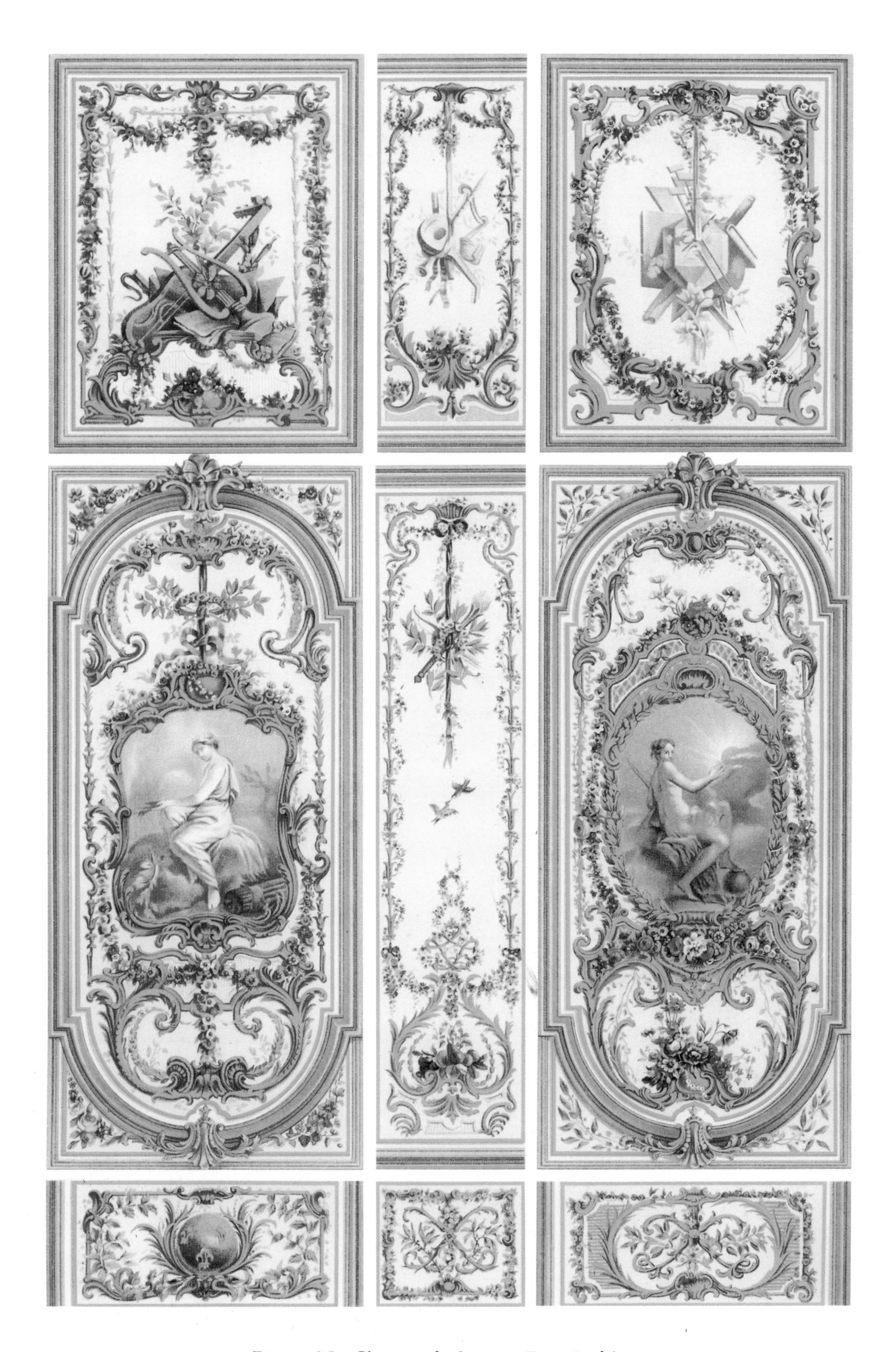

PLATE 35. Chateau de Sceaux, Fontainebleau

Plate 36. Wall decoration, Fontainebleau

PLATE 37. Salon des Singes, Chateau de Chantilly

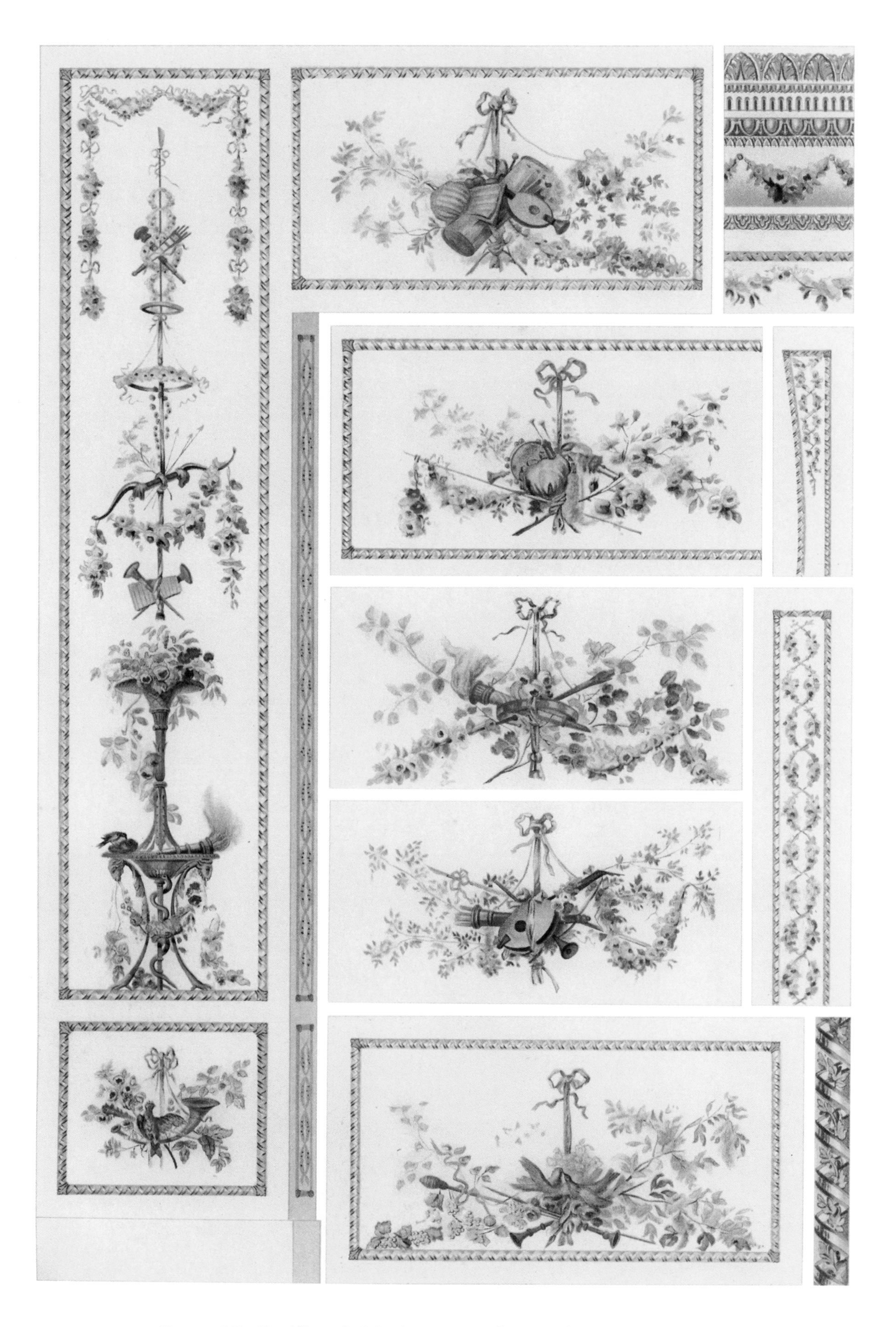

PLATE 38. Pavillon de Musique, Parc de Petit-Trianon, Versailles

PLATE 39. Ceiling painting, Spiegel Gallery, Versailles

PLATE 40. Gallery of Apollo, Louvre

PLATE 41. Hotel de Rohan [now Imprimerie Nationale]

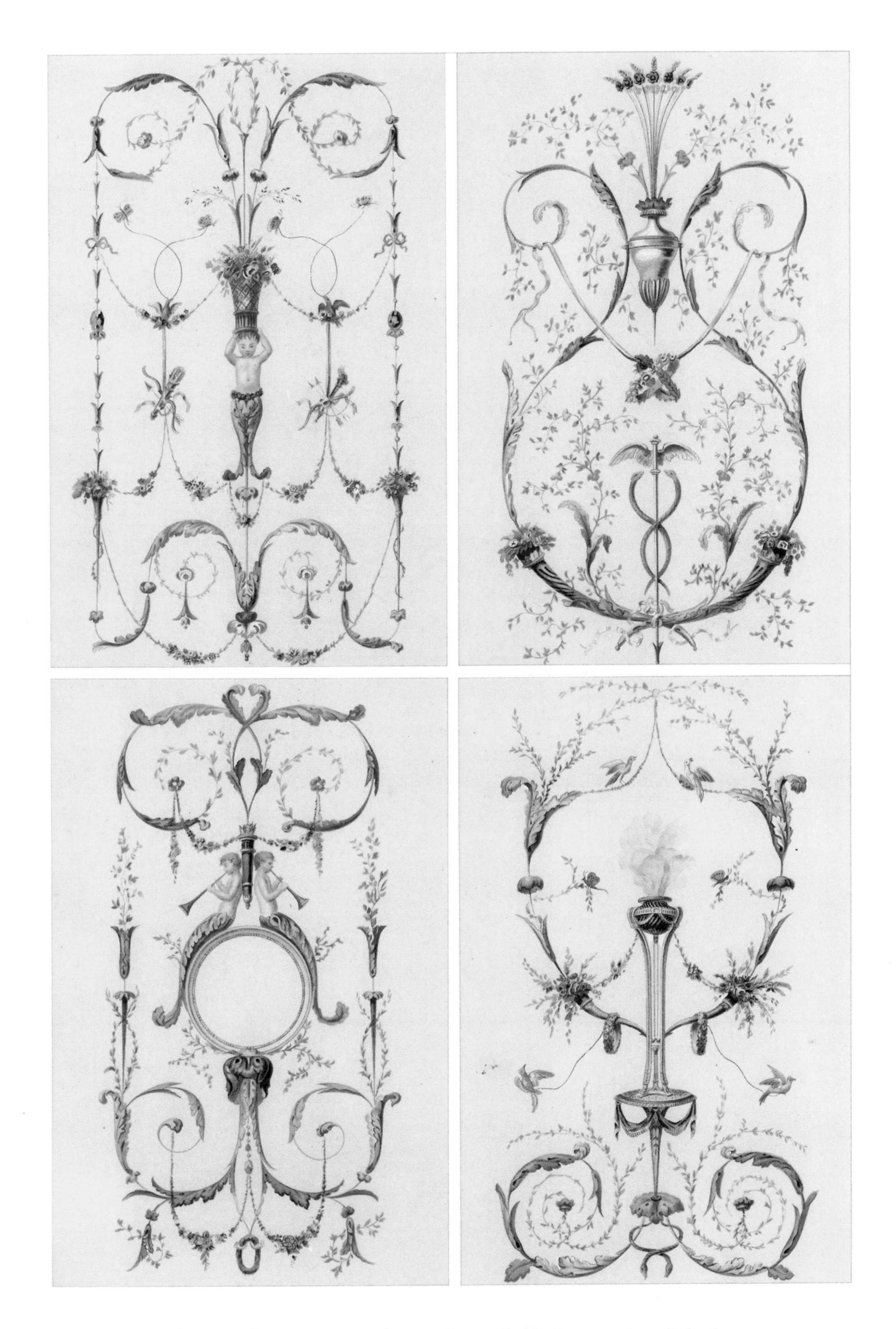

PLATE 42. From an unknown house in Paris, now demolished

PLATE 43. Museum of Decorative Arts, Paris

Plate 44. Cardinal's room, Chateau d'Ancy-le-Franc

Plate 45. Fireplace, Chateau d'Ecouen

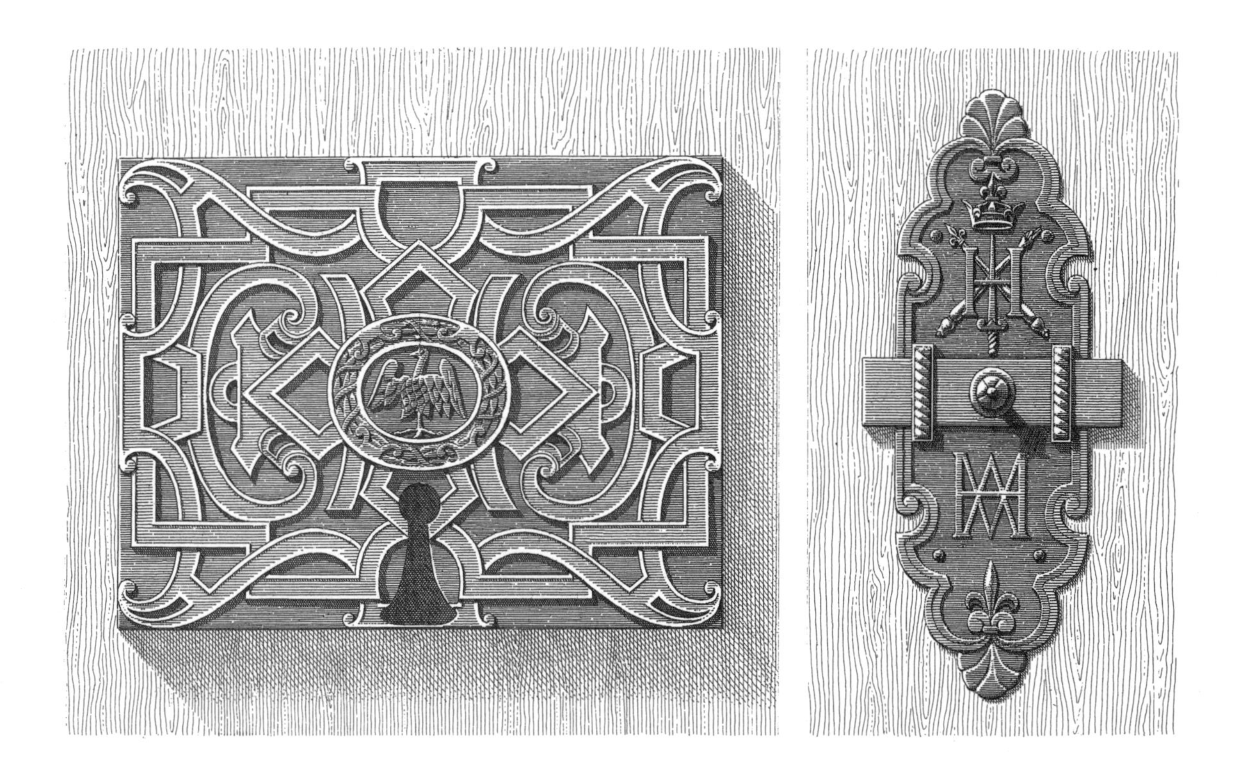

PLATE 46. Ironwork, Chateau d'Ecouen

Plate 47. Entrance door, Hotel de Vögüe

PLATE 48. Fireplace, Hotel de Vögüe

Plate 49. Ceiling of the Imperial Library

PLATE 50. Wall, Hotel de Sully

Plate 51. Fireplace of the king's bedroom, Chateau de Cheverny

PLATE 52. Great room of Parade, Hotel de Lauzun

PLATE 53. Alcove of the bedroom, Hotel de Lauzun

Plate 54. Fireplace wall in bedroom, Hotel de Lauzun

PLATE 55. Bedroom, Hotel de Lauzun

Plate 56. Doorway in the "Salle des Etats"

Plate 57. Door of the first courtroom

Plate 58. Door of the second courtroom

Plate 59. Fireplace wall

Plate 60. Grand fireplace, Lyon Town Hall

PLATE 61. Fireplace wall, Hotel d'Ormesson

Plate 62. Wall of entrance hall, Hotel d'Ormesson

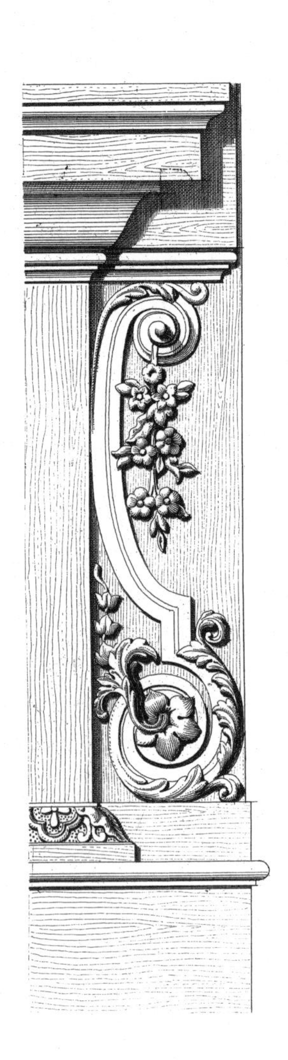

PLATE 63. Details, Hotel d'Ormesson

Plate 64. Paneling of salon on first floor, Chateau de Bercy

Plate 65. Paneling of salon on first floor, Chateau de Bercy

Plate 66. Mirror surmount, Chateau de Bercy

PLATE 67. Stone ceiling in the baptismal chapel, Church of Tillières

Plate 68. Stone ceiling of choir, Church of Tillières

PLATE 69. Stone ceiling of choir, Church of Tillières

PLATE 70. Entrance door

Plate 71. Painted wood ceiling, Musée de Cluny

PLATE 72. Room, Chateau de Rambouillet

PLATE 73. Fireplace, Chateau de Rambouillet

PLATE 74. Door, wall panel, and window, Chateau de Rambouillet

PLATE 75. Door and wall panel, Chateau de Rambouillet

PLATE 76. Cove above a window, Chateau de Rambouillet

Plate 77. Mirror wall in bedroom of the Princess de Rohan, Hotel de Soubise

Plate 78. Plan of one section of oval in grand salon of Princess de Rohan, Hotel de Soubise

PLATE 79. Ceiling design for salon of Princess de Rohan, Hotel de Soubise

Plate 80. Detail of carved panel for salon of Princess de Rohan, Hotel de Soubise

Plate 81. Salon of Minister of Public Works, Paris

PLATE 82. Mirror and fireplace, salon of Minister of Public Works, Paris

Plate 83. Doorway, salon of Minister of Public Works, Paris

PLATE 84. Detail of mirror, salon of Minister of Public Works, Paris

PLATE 85. Queen Marie Antoinette's boudoir, Petit Trianon

Plate 86. Doorway, Petit Trianon

PLATE 87. Mirror surmount in salon on ground floor, General Post Office, Paris

PLATE 88. Rose design in ceiling, General Post Office, Paris

PLATE 89. Wall, Hotel de Boufflers

PLATE 90. Design above the door, Hotel Vigier